THE HEART
OF
FEAR

A SURGEON'S COLLECTION OF STORIES
ON ADVERSITY, PASSION AND
PERSEVERANCE

ALEXANDRA KHARAZI, MD

 GLASSSPIDERPUBLISHING

To the people who shared their stories with me, offering a glimpse into their lives. This book is dedicated to you, with gratitude and admiration. May you continue to live boldly, pushing the limits of what's possible.

Contents

Part II

Acknowledgments

Thanks to the family and friends who have walked with me on this journey, and who have shown me that the heart of fear is also the heart of hope, of courage, and of possibility.

Thanks to my little girl, Harper, who reminds me every day of the beauty and wonder of the world around us.

Thanks to the road itself, leading me ever onward into the unknown, the impossible, the infinite.

Author's Note

Most of the doctors interviewed in this book have chosen to remain anonymous. But their silence speaks volumes, reminding us that the truth isn't always welcomed. Through my writing, I aim to create a safe space for conversations by allowing their voices to ring loud and clear. Because that is the catalyst for change— our ability to be honest, vulnerable, and authentic.

Introduction

The Heart of Fear is a journey into the raw and often untold emotions of fear and stress that permeate high-risk careers. As a practicing cardiothoracic surgeon, I have witnessed the effects of high-stress environments on my colleagues and friends. That's why I set out to capture their stories and give a voice to the countless others who have felt overwhelmed, burned out, and ineffective.

Through in-depth interviews with professionals in demanding fields, I explore the strategies and mindsets that allow individuals to thrive under pressure. From the operating room to skydiving, I share my own personal journey and the lessons I've learned about embracing opportunities often disguised as challenges.

Whether you're a medical professional seeking inspiration or someone who has felt overwhelmed by life's challenges, this book will provide you with valuable insights and a new perspective. It brings light to a universal truth we can all relate to. It's about the courage to jump, to let go of what holds us back, and to soar to new heights.

Part I

"Show me a hero and I'll write you a tragedy."
-F. Scott Fitzgerald

Chapter One: Overcoming the Weight of Expectations

Fear (noun): an unpleasant often strong emotion caused by anticipation or awareness of danger. (Merriam-Webster)

Zira* is no stranger to fear. Born and raised in Nigeria, he defied the odds when he came to the United States to pursue his education.

As the plane touched down on the tarmac, Zira's heart raced with anticipation. He'd left his home country behind with nothing but a one-way ticket and a dream of becoming a doctor in the United States.

Zira's mind drifted back to the hustle and bustle of Lagos, the city he once called home. The sounds of laughter and music filled the air in the colorful markets. He missed the aroma of his mother's jollof rice. He could almost smell it now, if he tried hard enough, in this cold and dreary airport. Though he yearned for that familiar comfort, he also felt grateful for the opportunity to begin his journey.

He pursued medicine to help others and serve his community. It seemed very simple at the time. He tackled medical school and residency with zest and an intense work ethic. Known for his kindness and gentle nature, Zira was well liked by coresidents and hospital staff.

After enduring the long hours and arduous training required to complete a cardiothoracic surgery fellowship, he became a practicing surgeon. He was excited to work in an underserved area in the Midwest, and he was eager to use his skills where they were most needed.

When he was hired for his first job out of training, Zira was told his role would be to bring a struggling cardiothoracic program into the twenty-first century. He dove in headfirst, operating on the sickest patients. But as he soon discovered, the world of medicine can be a cruel and unforgiving place.

He took on complex cases, often with limited resources. Analysis of his operative statistics showed that his outcomes were on par with the national average.

Success for a brand-new surgeon, right?

Wrong.

Professional jealousies began to arise, and scrutiny found him in the most unlikely places.

A malnourished patient with fragile lungs had a prolonged air leak after a lobectomy. Zira took the patient back to the operating room and appropriately managed the complication. Soon after, he was called to a meeting and harshly criticized by administrators who had minimal knowledge of thoracic surgery. It was demoralizing.

"It affected what I enjoyed most—going to the OR. Fixing hearts with my hands," he shares. "It robbed me of my joy."

The environment felt dangerous, even paralyzing. It began to impact his personal life. It left him feeling anxious, isolated, and overwhelmed.

"It affected my ability to be present," he recalls. "I would be playing with my son one minute, and then become distracted. That's time I won't get back, and it adds up."

He started to work from a place of fear. Fear of adverse outcomes and not having support. Fear of scrutiny. The fear eroded his confidence in doing the work that had once brought him so much joy. He was less inclined to take on challenging cases or offer heroic measures. He strayed far from his original goal of helping others, erecting a wall to protect himself. He was less inclined to take risks, even if it meant fighting for his patients.

Previously fearless, practicing medicine now filled Zira with dread. Until the day it all became too much. It was then that Zira discovered fear can be a catalyst for change.

"I woke up in the morning and I quit my job. That was it. There was no joy left. I felt unappreciated. Unwelcome."

Zira was angry and bitter. Most of all, he felt betrayed by the system that was supposed to help him succeed. It was the opposite of job security. After twenty-two years of education, he contemplated his worst-case scenario: The thought that he might have to develop a new skill set.

Would he be able to support his family? His aging parents?

Taking the plunge was scary. He hit rock bottom and began again.

He started with locum jobs full of skepticism, but to his surprise, he was welcomed. A locum is a medical professional who steps in to provide medical services when there is a staff shortage or a rapidly growing need not accommodated by existing resources. It was here that he was able to regain his confidence and his love of medicine.

He faced a similar complication with a prolonged air leak, but this time he was congratulated on his successful management of the patient.

"I liked the way I felt when I helped others," he tells me, recalling his first few months as a new surgeon.

How did Zira overcome his fear?

After leaving his first job, he gained perspective through introspection.

"Even in failure, I did the best I could. That's all any of us could do."

Reflecting on his experience, he simply says, "Mentally, it wasn't good," describing how his negative mindset affected his ability to care for his patients, his family, and his life.

Zira's story highlights the damaging effects that fear can have on one's life and work. It shows how fear can cloud our judgment and hold us back from pursuing our goals and overcoming obstacles. Through his determination and unwavering faith in himself, he was able to turn his anxieties about leaving a job that was seemingly "secure" into fuel to begin anew. Through Zira's journey, we can see how important it is to face our fears and strive to optimize our ability to make a positive impact in our own lives and find where we are most needed in our communities.

The obvious question we're left with is this: How can we temper external factors by going within ourselves to find peace?

Chapter Two: From Struggle to Strength, an Inner Revolution

Katherine* left the glitz and glam of a career in the music industry to pursue medicine. She describes herself as ambitious, committed, and a go-getter. She had no trouble surpassing the initial milestones, breezing through the MCAT and medical school. She discovered a passion for neurosurgery, so she pursued it with vigor and fierce determination.

Unfortunately, Katherine landed in a completely unsupportive and malignant residency program where she was quickly singled out.

"I practiced in a way that was compassionate and thorough," she tells me.

These attributes were not valued by her program. She continued to be criticized for inefficiency, spending too long talking to families, and seeing "medical" consults. Other doctors in the hospital took notice, praising her for her compassionate care. Still, the target on her back was palpable.

"They built a rocky stage with no support," she says.

Once she was singled out, it was one thing after another. She describes herself as the scapegoat. To make matters worse, she became aware of two preliminary candidates who were a better fit for her program. The faculty seemed keen to replace her. Her confidence plummeted.

The turning point came when Katherine was asked to perform a challenging procedure. Her patient was a baby who had cerebrospinal fluid leaking from her spinal cord. Katherine was asked to place a lumbar drain, a procedure that involves inserting a small tube into the lower part of the back near the spine to collect and drain the leaking fluid. This procedure relieves pressure around the brain and spinal cord.

Although Katherine had an ICU attending physician with her, she inadvertently entered the inferior vena cava. Immediately, the error was recognized and a vascular surgeon was consulted. Ultimately, the medical team pulled the drain and held pressure. The vascular surgeon comforted her.

"Everyone makes mistakes," the surgeon told Katherine. "The right thing was done to manage the complication. The baby will be fine."

The baby was fine. But Katherine wasn't.

"I knew as soon as it happened, I would be fired over this," she recalls.

She was right. She was called to a meeting and given a choice to be let go or to resign. She chose the latter and handed in her resignation letter.

She says she could have reported the program for multiple atrocities.

"I've seen my colleagues make mistakes that resulted in bad outcomes and not bear the same harsh consequences that I had to," she confides. "But I had worked too hard, and exposing them could have meant the end of my career."

After the meeting, feelings of anxiety and fear mounted. Following her experience, Katherine was diagnosed with PTSD by a psychiatrist, and she began treatment.

Luckily, others in the hospital recognized her hard work and considered her an exceptional physician. This led to an unexpected opportunity to change paths and pursue a career as an anesthesiologist.

Once Katherine secured her career transition,

something amazing happened. Her mindset shifted. She felt she had nothing to lose.

"I realized the worst had happened. I was not going to be a neurosurgeon. I felt like a failure. So I said 'I no longer want to impress anyone. I'm just here for the patients.' "

Katherine resolved to spend the remaining months in her program making a positive difference in the lives of those around her. The impostor syndrome she had developed lessened when she was no longer concerned with what others thought of her or what "might happen" as a result of those opinions.

She was back to her original goal. She became emboldened. She took all the time she needed in family meetings. She stood up publicly for her junior residents.

"I opted to give them a good environment. The program was built to knock residents down, but I focused on their strengths. It made them better."

Her process improvement had a direct and tangible effect. When errors were made, she focused on the facts and the process. She was among the first in her institution to enforce time-outs during bedside procedures. This followed an error for which a resident was personally blamed and shamed.

Katherine went on to pursue an anesthesiology fellowship at a prestigious Ivy League university.

What did she learn?

"The key to success is they make you believe in yourself. Focusing on people's strengths makes them do better."

Her new environment changed her mindset. She compared it to her first experience.

"We get beat up, and we beat people up, and they get shaky," she shares. "It's bad for patient care."

Changing her perspective made Katherine a better physician. She struggled to do what was right for patients in a malignant environment that didn't align with her moral values. She then changed her environment and applied her signature strengths, which were now recognized as assets. This allowed her to focus on her anesthesiology practice without worrying about failure. She stopped allowing anxiety and fear to influence her decisions.

"I wasn't walking on eggshells anymore."

Katherine's journey highlights the importance of perseverance and self-discovery.

Despite facing numerous challenges and obstacles, she never lost sight of her identity and continued to strive toward her goals.

Through her inner transformation, she learned to embrace her imperfections and flaws and discovered her true strength, showing us the resilience of the human spirit in its war with adversity.

Katherine's story can serve as an inspiration for anyone working through their own challenges to keep striving toward their goals. By embracing imperfections and focusing on self-discovery, we can find the strength to triumph over hardship and transform our lives for the better.

Chapter Three: Managing Fear and Anxiety in Medical Practice

Jennifer* is really good at her job. She's an ophthalmologist who's known for her unwavering dedication to her patients, clinical expertise, and efficiency.

Her colleagues appreciate her quick wit and genuine interest in their lives. At home, she's a self-described "hot mess," juggling the demands of her career with parenting her two toddlers and chasing the ever-elusive work-life balance.

I interview Jennifer on a Tuesday afternoon between my cases. The conversation between us flows easily. She's a friend. We've known each other since college. We bonded over hot Cheetos and Gatorade during late-night study sessions at the library. We've come a long way. I want to hear her story from the beginning.

"It was watching my dad in a downward spiral," she says.

Her father's lung cancer motivated her to pursue a career in medicine.

"He was in pretty good health," she explains, "and he declined quickly. It made me want to impact people's day-to-day lives. Find meaning in my work."

There were other factors. Jennifer grew up poor.

"Medicine is a well-respected career with a steady income. I could provide for my family," she tells me.

Many of us pursue medicine for its versatility. Patient care, research, and administrative opportunities, to name a few. The traditional path is well paved. For most of us, it starts in college, where we take pre-med courses. Once the requirements are completed, we take the MCAT. From there we go to medical school, residency, fellowship.

From the time we enter medical school, there is an average of seven to ten years of additional training before becoming "attending" physicians. Before we've "made it," so to speak. This path is fraught with challenges.

Jennifer took some time after college to work at Facebook before she embarked on her calling.

"Medicine is a heavy field," she tells me. "It's life

and death. I knew I wanted to make a difference on an individual level, but I wanted to be sure medicine was the right path."

Once she got into medical school, she smoothly careened through the milestones. She got one of the highest scores in her class on the USMLE Step 1 exam. She describes it as an isolating and intense experience, despite achieving her goal.

"Each one of these steps, in a way determines your destiny."

In Jennifer's case, this was literally true. During the residency match, applicants often have little control over where they end up for residency training. Jennifer didn't match in her city and was forced to choose between her family and her career.

"We were apart for four years," she tells me. "It was a lot. I had a baby."

Not being able to train in the same city as her family despite all her hard work was demoralizing—but, like many of us, she pressed on.

The fear starts early and then builds.

"That I won't score well on the MCAT, won't match, won't find a job," she tells me. "It takes different forms along the path."

I can relate. We are all familiar with some version of

anticipating failure.

Today, Jennifer has it all. She is a practicing ophthalmologist in a coveted Southern California multi-specialty group. For her, work-life balance is an ongoing journey. She loves her job but prioritizes what matters most, spending time with her kids and stay-at-home husband.

From the outside, things look great. But are they really? Like most cases, there's more to this story.

"The fear, the dread," she tells me, "sometimes it literally makes me sick to my stomach."

The root of her fear? The possibility of a lawsuit. The possibility her group will decide not to keep her as a partner. Losing her medical license, reputation, and livelihood that she has worked so hard to achieve.

She practices more conservatively for medico-legal reasons.

And on a personal note, she stopped rock climbing.

"I do procedures. I can't risk injuring my hands. At the end of the day, I need to pay the bills."

How does she cope?

"All I can do is my best. Not allow fear to trigger me. Come to terms with it."

Jennifer describes fear as a personal prison that physicians often create for themselves. Her story highlights the many fears that can accompany a career in medicine, from the pressure of exams to the anxieties of practice.

It's a reminder that, even as we overcome one challenge, new issues will inevitably arise and bring with them fresh fears and insecurities. However, we can choose to view these as opportunities.

Jennifer's story also provides a glimpse of hope. She copes with her fears by focusing on what she can control, and doing her best. Her resilience and determination serve as evidence that coming to terms with our fears gives us the courage to keep going in the face of uncertainty.

To put these lessons into inspired action, we can turn our attention to negative and limiting thoughts. We can challenge and reframe these thoughts to generate positive, empowering beliefs.

Chapter Four: The Practice of Reframing - Understanding How Our Thoughts Shape Our Reality

Laura Fortner is a board-certified OBGYN and certified career coach based in rural Ohio. With over twenty-one years of experience in the field, she has seen it all—from private practice to her current role as an OB hospitalist. However, several years ago, her career was thrown into turmoil when she was hit with a multimillion-dollar malpractice lawsuit. She lost. Despite her extensive medical expertise, she found herself struggling with a host of negative emotions like shame, anger, fear, and self-doubt. But Laura is not one to give up easily.

I met Laura after being served with my first medical malpractice lawsuit. The statistics are stark. If you practice in a high-risk specialty and work to the age of sixty-five, you have a ninety-nine percent chance of being sued. That number falls to seventy-five percent for practitioners in a low-risk specialty.

My introduction to the legal world came early.

Losing a patient after a difficult case is devastating. Most of us are ill-prepared to deal with the legal consequences. Patients and families often don't know the difference between negligence and a bad outcome. The court system becomes part of the grieving process.

The papers arrived at my office on a Wednesday. The first line read "You have been sued." By that time, most of us would have pieced it together through the unsavory experience of being served. But just in case you aren't sure, there it is in black and white.

After four years of medical school, five years of general surgery training, and two years of fellowship, I realized I knew nothing about malpractice lawsuits.

Once my malpractice insurance company assigned me a lawyer, he was able to break down the legal terminology. He explained the process of discovery, obtaining an expert witness, and depositions. Yet I still felt lost navigating my new reality.

I heard about Laura through word of mouth. I had never heard of a malpractice coach, and I figured she would help me bridge the gap between medical and legal. I pictured getting helpful tips preparing for depositions and trial.

Laura is open about her story. In the midst of dealing with her lawsuit, she sought help and invested in a life coach to understand her thoughts and overcome negative emotions that were holding her back. Her newfound peace of mind inspired her to help other physicians facing similar challenges. She now works one-on-one with her clients, helping them to find their purpose, joy, and peace of mind. Laura is passionate about her work and is confident she can help anyone who needs it.

"In a way, the best thing that ever happened to me was being sued," she tells me, speaking from the vantage point of her thriving coaching business. She continues to work as an ob-gyn. Now, patient care brings her joy.

You can tell she loves what she does. Laura helps people be at peace regardless of the outcome. She no longer makes decisions from a place of fear.

Laura had to shed preconceived notions to change her thinking and heal herself. Now she helps others.

"Fear-based conditioning starts early in our training," she shares. "We essentially purchase medical school, and for many of us, we are invested, we can't leave. The fear-based culture starts at this point and goes forward. We tell ourselves we cannot go elsewhere. We believe that good grades, hard work, and grit will get us there."

I nod my head as she speaks, for this is the dream we are sold as medical students. Many continue even though they are dissatisfied.

"Hindsight is 20/20," Laura tells me when I mention this thought. "I look back at the people who decided not to continue when they reached that point, and I consider them brave. Most of us override that."

She continues to describe the downward spiral.

"Negative thoughts start to circle," she says. "We find evidence to support those thoughts."

Laura tells me she has clients who pick careers out of fear. The notion that there is less likelihood of being sued in a low-risk specialty pushes people toward those fields they perceive as low-risk.

Fear also encroaches in other ways.

"People believe they are not smart, not good enough, not technically skilled," Laura continues. She helps rewire that thinking and dispel those myths.

Through her journey, Laura turned her pain into purpose. Her lawsuit had the worst possible outcome, and it allowed her to transcend the fear she had been conditioned to believe since her training.

Laura isn't scared anymore.

"It's a process," she tells me. "It has to be taught. It's creating a new narrative."

I recall walking into the surgeons' lounge and mentioning my own lawsuit. We are advised not to discuss the details of the case, but we can share our experiences. I mentioned it openly, and most people in the room chimed in about their malpractice encounters.

So why aren't more of us talking about it? The culture of shame in medicine. The intentional and covert isolation is often propagated through our training. Our egos create images of us that we believe will be shattered if our colleagues and patients "find out" who we are.

"This is the core of fear-based thinking," Laura says. "In a way, most people have impostor syndrome, and they're afraid they are not as good as everyone thinks they are, and their image will disintegrate.

"We literally are told that we are allowed to do no harm," she brings as an example, citing the Hippocratic oath, "but nobody is perfect, and when patients are very sick, bad things can happen no matter what we do. Shifting your mindset involves uncovering limiting thoughts and beliefs that have been deeply ingrained."

I ask for an example of a mindset shift.

"It can be so simple. You think it won't work, but it does."

Laura recalls working with a client on changing the narrative from "I have to do all these things" to "I *get* to do all these things."

Laura shows us a path to resilience through self-discovery. Through her journey, she has overcome the immense challenges of a malpractice lawsuit and rediscovered her purpose and joy as a physician and career coach. Her passion for helping other doctors find peace and fulfillment in the midst of hardship reminds us that there is always the possibility of transformation and renewal. Progress often finds us disguised as discomfort. Hard lessons. Internal and external conflict.

Her journey is a powerful example of how we can use our thoughts as tools to create our desired reality. Just like Laura's negative thoughts were holding her back and causing her to feel helpless, when she changed her perspective and invested in her personal growth, she was able to overcome her challenges.

Her story teaches us it's possible to harness the power of our thoughts and beliefs to create a life that aligns with our goals and desires. By taking control of our thoughts and focusing on growth, we can unlock our full potential and become the best version of ourselves.

Chapter Five: Finding Joy in the Journey

"**W**hy do you wear so much makeup?" Olivia's* classmate asked her point-blank. It was hard not to notice her. Her bold makeup and edgy wardrobe choices were a stark contrast to the white lab coats and sensible shoes of her peers. Olivia was in her first year of medical school. Her classmate seemed surprised. He was trying to make sense of why and how she'd achieved the same milestones as he. She didn't embody what he believed a doctor "should" look like. Yet her fiery determination fueled her non-conventional approach to life and her studies. It was palpable.

In the present day, Olivia is an interventional cardiologist in a metropolitan city. By all accounts, she is highly accomplished. What's most captivating about her is her humor and heart.

"I could go to a club and dance one day, and read

EKGs the next!" she laughs.

"Medicine is self-selective," she tells me. "People are driven but conservative."

She cites the common dream of achieving the "destination" by becoming an attending physician. This is what's called the arrival fallacy: the thought that achieving the "destination" will bring happiness.

Happiness research shows us that's not the case. The brain quickly adjusts to a new "set point."

For medical students, the arrival fallacy is often becoming an attending physician, and, as Olivia puts it, "Having two children in a dual-income household, putting money into a retirement account, and discussing real estate investments in Facebook groups."

Is that even the dream anymore? The stability that a career in medicine has been traditionally known for is wavering. Often, doctors are being hired by senior, more established physicians. Hospitals are hiring doctors. Contracts can be interrupted on a whim.

Even for those who manage to hold out on their own, insurance reimbursements are dwindling, and practice expenses and malpractice costs are climbing. Autonomy is decreasing, and satisfaction is plummeting. There is the prevailing feeling that for as much as was invested, the outcome is modest. Many mourn what was "given up" along the way.

Olivia is different because she gave nothing up. She traveled, learned multiple languages, and made friends all over the world. She worked in labs and sampled various careers. She took time off while in medical school and moved to Switzerland. She became a Fulbright scholar. Every step of her journey brought her joy.

Now she has "arrived." Her job satisfaction soars because her experiences are what brought her to this point in life.

What is her biggest fear?

She tells me about a trauma patient she encountered who tragically suffered a high cervical spine fracture and ended up a quadriplegic.

"It's loss of physical and psychological autonomy. Losing my voice," she says.

How does that translate to the possibility of losing her career?

"I would just leave through the same door I came," she tells me with that familiar laugh.

Humor is one of Olivia's signature strengths. Despite the hardships in her life, she has the uncanny ability to make light of any situation.

"Other career options?" I ask.

"Maybe politics. Yeah, politics."

I can tell she's speaking off the cuff. The possibility doesn't occur to her because she doesn't fear it. What's important is that she has her voice.

She confirms my thoughts are true.

"Medicine is not my identity," she tells me. "There's sort of a freedom to that."

Olivia chose a highly specialized field because she wanted to feel like she was making a difference through tangible results. She loves what she does. But because she is confident of her intrinsic value, she knows she would find that happiness again.

"My self-worth, my value, is so much more than what I do in medicine. More than rounding every day, or even my high-risk cases in the lab."

She knows she has more to give than that, and maybe we all should.

"The value I have for myself, that's how I got to medicine," Olivia explains. "I don't look at medicine to define my value."

The proverbial "it's the journey," I say.

"Not losing sight of who you are," she adds. "Asking yourself who you are. Recognizing who you are, and choosing your path."

So, what can we learn from Olivia's journey to apply to our own lives? First, it's essential to reflect on our own values and beliefs to make sure they align with our chosen career path. Next, we should strive to maintain our sense of self and not let our careers define us. Finally, we can work on actively welcoming change, life's only certainty, whether that means seeking new experiences or letting go of our resistance to the ever-evolving landscape of our circumstances. Instead of being victim to our circumstances, can we reframe them and learn to view them differently.

By focusing on the path instead of fixating solely on the destination, can we find opportunity in the wake of the unexpected explosions?

Chapter Six: The Lone Wolf - One Surgeon's Fight for Autonomy and Patient-Centered Care

Mike* gets into trouble a lot.

He is known to be confrontational and antagonistic, and often comes across as offensive.

He agreed to speak with me.

I ask him, "Why medicine?"

Mike's path to becoming a surgeon started with a chance encounter when he was in the infantry Marine Corps. A soldier got shot and was brought to the trauma bay. Mike was a bystander, but the trauma surgeon didn't know that. He started assigning Mike tasks while he expeditiously opened the chest. Mike went with the flow. He found himself drawn to the excitement and challenge of saving a life.

The concept of my book is a tough sell for Mike. He

partially agrees with the premise, but not entirely. He believes external factors out of our control influence fear.

"People often act out of fear of not being compliant," he tells me, "anticipating scrutiny."

This causes many to order unnecessary tests "to be safe." Patient complications and medical bills run high. Business as usual in health care.

"No one wants to risk the liability," he adds.

Mike, an older surgeon, discusses his early days as a general surgeon. He was among the first to attempt laparoscopic lysis of adhesions with bowel obstructions. Patients do better in the long run with less intra-abdominal scar formation.

At the time, he was criticized heavily for this decision, even receiving a letter of discipline. He describes it as being "attacked by other surgeons." Despite criticism and opposition from his peers, he pressed on in his pursuit of medical excellence.

Mike is a fighter. He describes feelings of defensiveness. Despite the pushback, Mike continued to act in the best interests of the patients, refusing to acquiesce to administrative pressure.

"If I conformed, I would be disgusted with myself," he says.

One of Mike's patients, a middle-aged woman named Sarah*, came to him complaining of abdominal pain and bloating. After conducting a physical exam and reviewing her medical history, Mike suspected that she might have an abdominal mass and ordered a CT scan. However, the CT scan was unable to provide a definitive diagnosis.

Mike refused to accept the inconclusive results and knew that an MRI was the best way to accurately diagnose the issue. Unfortunately, MRI services weren't available at this community hospital at the time. Despite objections from the hospital administration, who argued that the patient should be kept in the hospital for further observation, Mike discharged Sarah and sent her out to get an MRI at a facility where it was available.

The results showed that Sarah had a rare abdominal tumor that could only be accurately diagnosed through an MRI. With this knowledge, Mike was able to create a customized treatment plan that led to successful removal of the tumor. By defying the hospital's protocols and sending Sarah for an MRI, Mike's independent thinking saved her life.

His willingness to go against the grain highlights the importance of thinking critically and always putting the patient first, inspiring us to do the same.

Now in solo practice, Mike believes that independence is crucial to his ability to be a good physician.

He admits he brings more friction to his life than necessary. Reportedly, he is very loyal to those who have earned his respect.

He tells me he is an expert at his craft. He particularly enjoys hernia operations and boasts of excellent results. He is known as a good technician, but a wild card.

"People may think I do the same operation every day, but really, I am getting better and better at what I do," he says, and I believe him. I've seen him operate.

While Mike is known for his technical proficiency, his approach to medicine is not without its controversies. He has a disdain for authority and is not afraid to challenge the status quo.

"My goal is to fix expectedly curable disease," he says simply.

Mike is a physician in solo practice, a dying breed. Most doctors are hired by hospitals and groups and have essentially become employees, which, according to Mike, is a mechanistic stumbling block. He's not one to mince words.

"They are wage earners. They lost their agency, loyal no longer to a patient but a paycheck."

His vantage point relies solely on physicians being independent. In the current era, that may mean the willingness to move around and change jobs—likening it to the paradigm of independence in tech.

"There's a healthiness to that," he says, "not being bound to an organization."

He also emphasizes needing less. Living within modest means.

I ask him about inner dialogue. Does he criticize himself? Does he have self-compassion? When it comes to his inner thoughts, Mike is surprisingly self-reserved.

Mike tells me he has no self-talk at all, and no internal conversations. At least none he is willing to share either on or off the record.

"During the tedious part of a difficult case," he tells me, "I find myself drawn to random memories."

"Like what?" I ask.

"A sudden recollection of the way they serve pizza in the eighth grade."

"A different time?" I offer. "Like during times of stress, you go to times of comfort, seeking stability to regain your composure?"

"I don't know if I would go that far," he cuts in, shutting the conversation down.

I wonder if this is the effect of being part of an older generation of surgeons—an inability to come to terms with years of trauma and process it in a healthy way.

Nonetheless, he embodies the qualities of an independent thinker, unafraid to challenge the status quo and pave his own path to better patient outcomes. He is an inspiration to those discouraged by the rigidness of traditional systems who value a more human-centered approach to healthcare.

Part II

"We don't see things as they are, we see them as we
are."
-Anais Nin

Chapter Seven: When Plans Change - Lessons learned from Skydiving and Surgery

E ach step is calculated.

Each step is deliberate.

Each step is taken with the goal of saving a life.

Everyone needs a hobby, but skydiving can expose you to precarious scenarios. When you're in a high-stress situation, your training kicks in. You do what you need to do to regain control, deploy your reserve, and fly your canopy to safety. The same goes for a high-stress situation in the operating room. Your training kicks in.

You do what you need to do to save the life of your patient.

You do what you need to do to fix the problem.

It's interesting that the mindset I learned from

skydiving has translated to my career as a physician. In both skydiving and medicine, you have to be able to think on your feet and make quick

decisions under pressure. You need to be confident in your abilities but also humble enough to acknowledge that there is always room for growth.

Both require a commitment to safety and attention to detail. The consequences of a mistake in either skydiving or medicine can be severe, so it's important to always be vigilant and proactive in identifying and addressing potential issues. It's a great feeling when everything goes smoothly and the end result is a successful jump or a successful operation. But what do we do when things go wrong?

I was first exposed to skydiving when I was a medical student. There was a drop zone forty-five minutes north of the medical school campus. The training came naturally to me because it was similar to medical training in many ways.

The training started with the accelerated freefall program, or AFF. This consisted of a ground school and a written test on the logistics of skydiving. Next was a series of competencies that need to be demonstrated in the air.

I began with two instructors, downgraded to one,

and then was released on my own. The maneuvers were meant to demonstrate stability in the air and the ability to regain control in an unstable position during free fall.

Barrel roll.

Simple flip.

The second part of the jump consisted of parachute deployment and canopy piloting. Once the parachute is safely overhead, the focus shifts to flying the landing pattern—landing into the wind, and safely.

The most critical portion of the training is learning the emergency procedures. A skydiving rig consists of a main canopy, a reserve canopy, in some cases an automatic activation device, and a reserve static line which is designed to automatically deploy the reserve parachute after the main canopy is cut away.

I learned the emergency procedures. I learned my gear inside and out. I learned about the plethora of malfunctions, the most common of which is line twists. One of the least common malfunctions is two parachutes out. I studied these malfunctions and learned how to deal with them quickly. In theory.

When the day my first malfunction came, it was my fourth skydive of the day. It was jump number one hundred twenty-eight. I had a successful three-way free fall with two friends. We waved to each other before we split, and flew our separate ways.

At thirty-five hundred feet, I pulled out my pilot chute. Under normal circumstances, this dislodges the closing pin and opens the container, deploying the main parachute. Except mine didn't come out.

I turned behind me to see the pilot chute flapping in the air. I reached back and tried to manually pull on it and open the main container.

Now I was down to three-thousand feet. It wasn't coming out. I kept trying.

Twenty-five hundred feet. My audible altimeter was beeping louder and louder. There was still no canopy above my head. I couldn't get my main chute out.

I pulled my reserve handle. It was a rough opening, but there it was: my blue-and-white reserve canopy. I flew it down.

After my feet hit the ground, the emotions set in.

Relief.

Fear.

"That was a close call."

So what happened?

I talked to the rigger at the drop zone, then to several friends and jump partners. Most likely, it was faulty packing on my part. Mistakes are unavoidable. Predictable, even. What matters is dealing with them when they inevitably arise.

The importance of knowing emergency procedures cannot be overstated, as they can mean the difference between success and failure.

One Monday morning, I was scheduled to do bypass surgery but got called urgently to the cath lab for a different patient. The patient was originally brought to the cath lab for a STEMI (ST Elevation Myocardial Infarction), otherwise known as a heart attack. After further evaluation, the cardiologist discovered the patient was actually suffering from a Type A aortic dissection.

The patient was awake on the cath lab table. His name was John*. I walked in and told him that this was a surgical emergency and I would have to replace the ascending aorta. I explained to him that to do this, I would have to open his chest, put him on cardiopulmonary bypass, and arrest the heart. This operation would also require deep hypothermic circulatory arrest, where we would cool the body to take off the cross-clamp.

As you can imagine, the patient was shocked. I asked him what family he had. He told me it was him, his wife, and their baby girl. She was the same age as my little girl, Harper, who was almost two at the time.

The operation itself went well. I was able to sew in the graft. After multiple blood products, we were finally ready to close the patient's chest.

We took him back to the ICU. I went to the call room to get some rest. It had been an eight-hour operation. About thirty minutes after arrival at the ICU, at around three a.m., I heard a Code Blue overhead in his room. His heart was fibrillating. The ICU team tried to defibrillate with external pads unsuccessfully.

Quickly, I opened the chest at the bedside. I looked up at the monitor as I was removing the sternal wires. Asystole.

Shit. Come on, John.

I started cardiac massage. The heart came back. We started pacing.

I left the chest open that night and brought him back the next day to close him.

He eventually made it out of the hospital and saw his little girl again.

Looking back, I recognized that what was going through my head at the time was very similar to a malfunction during a skydive. I had to do what needed to be done to save my patient's life.

There was no panic.

Everything moves in slow motion when I'm in a situation like this.

I take a deep breath and act.

Chapter Eight: Nine Lives and Counting - The Doctor who Jumps Off Buildings for Fun

Charley Kurlinkus is an emergency room doctor in Sacramento, California. He has been working nights in the emergency department.

One night, there was a multiple police officer gunshot wound alert. He describes an officer, still in his uniform. At first, Charley didn't see the entry wound in his neck.

"He was dead already," Charley tells me.

He immediately took control of the room. Several of the victim's fellow officers were watching.

What was going through his mind?

It was simply, "I am here right now."

Charley and his team intubated the officer, established access, and continued resuscitating him. He did not survive. Charley recalls having to tell the officer's wife. That part of his job is hard but important.

He specializes in brief, intense situations. He does his best under the highest pressure. He thrives with the adrenaline most people attribute to stress.

Charley became interested in medicine from a young age, sparked during outdoor adventure camps. He describes lifeguarding and first aid. Eventually, he became an EMT. He describes it as a "weird job to have," but from my perspective, it suits him well.

He likes helping people in a bad situation, on the worst day of their lives, when he's on call at two a.m. And he's good at it.

"You have to have the ability to put stuff behind you."

Easier said than done.

The most powerful thing Charley said to me during our interview was, "Unfounded confidence has gotten me everything I have in life. I always believed that I can do stuff, and I have."

A seasoned BASE jumper, Charley also has nine lives. BASE jumping is when a person jumps from the top of a building, bridge, cliff, or other high place using a parachute. Usually, BASE jumpers jump from a height of a thousand feet or less. Compared to skydiving, the distance is shorter, the stakes are higher, and the rig has no reserve parachute. It's easier to acquire injuries, and mortality rates are higher. It's not a sport for the faint of heart

"I used to say I was 'invincible until proven otherwise.' "

He stopped saying that because of the number of friends he lost BASE jumping—which begs the obvious question: Does BASE jumping still scare him?

"It depends on the jump. If it's a brand-new object, yes. Jumping off something for the first time it's always scary."

He references a regular object he jumps from for fun, which doesn't evoke that same type of fear.

I want to know about his scariest situation.

"There was only one situation I thought I was going to die."

He describes a three-way jump off the 900-foot-high KL Tower in Kuala Lumpur.

Ironically, the jump was to spread the ashes of another jumper who had died during a jump.

Charley pitched his pilot chute early and became entangled with his friend's parachute, who was flying with a camera close by.

I imagined what he may have been thinking in his final moments, plummeting toward the ground at high speed. What would I be thinking?

But Charley just did what he always did. He did his best in a lousy situation. There was not a lot of time from a height of nine-hundred feet.

A bystander describes it best. "You looked like you were just flying your canopy."

It was the only thing left. Charley braced himself. And then he fell.

"I remember thinking this is gonna hurt."

After the impact, it was clear from his chest deformity that he had broken his ribs.

"I laid there, and I heard sirens. I remember thinking, oh shit, those are for me." He laughs.

One thing he can't recall is whether or not he felt fear.

So what drives him in BASE jumping and racing cars?

"I enjoy the nervous tension, the five seconds beforehand."

It's not lack of fear. He transforms fear into action. Repackages fear into power.

The key to his mindset? "You have to be willing to accept possible risk. Not perseverate."

Regardless of circumstance, Charley's confidence does not waver.

"I just get up," he simply says.
And I think that says it all.

Chapter Nine: Daring to Live Intensely - A Journey of Risk and Renewal

The last thing Nicole Smith-Ludvik remembers from the day her luck ran out was the truck that T-boned her car at sixty miles an hour.

Up to that point in her life, she was a successful executive in corporate sales. But that day, life as she knew it was ripped away from her. Nicole was flown in critical condition to a Level 1 trauma center. She suffered a traumatic brain injury and multiple broken bones. Her prognosis was grim.

"It seems as if you had nothing more to lose," I tell her, alluding to the tragic death of her husband only a year prior to her car accident.

"On the contrary, I had everything to lose!" Nicole says emphatically. In that moment, she completely reframed the events as I'd interpreted them.

It took months and a multi-disciplinary team of doctors and physical therapists to help return her to baseline. The accident was a turning point. "My life shifted," she says. "I was always living off this idea of the future. Then I had this realization I needed to move away from the retirement perspective."

Following the accident and her recovery, Nicole left the world of corporate sales, immersing herself in skydiving with grit and tenacity, ascending to instructor, instructor evaluator, and ultimately, a stuntwoman.

She went through the accelerated freefall program and found solace and peace in the air.

"It's freedom," she says simply. "All the internal dialogue stops. You are fully focused on the moment." What she describes is akin to meditation.

She thinks that people who are drawn to extreme sports have trauma. "Part of it is a rush," she says, "the brain gets conditioned to the dopamine response. Everything I do is a calculated risk. What do I know about the equipment? Aircraft? Statistics?"

Risk assessment allows her to quickly act in the moment when she's outside her comfort zone.

She describes her famous Burj Khalifa stunt for Emirates airlines.

"Hi, Mom, I'm on top of the world!" Nicole says from the top of the earth's tallest building. I watch the footage on YouTube, and what strikes me most is that she looks happy. Calm.

"I want you to imagine this," she says. "The risk assessment is 130 pages. It includes assessment of the platform, the winds, how I would be attached, safety procedures, etcetera."

Climbing up onto the spire that day, she felt sweaty palms. She was anxious.

She recalls the safety protocols, the training, the plan.

"The mind is constantly thinking about what could go wrong."

Nicole challenges those thoughts, instead focusing on what can go right.

"I reminded myself I was attached in multiple places. I trained for this. Conditions were well selected, and I worked with a skilled team who put this together."

That's what fear means to Nicole. A mechanism by which the mind makes sense of the unknown. This creates anxiety.

The climb to the top of Burj Khalifa started an hour and a half before sunrise. It was familiar yet unknown.

Nicole was no stranger to heights. But she was a stranger to the absence of a parachute.

From this unique vantage point, Nicole found mindfulness. She processed her fear. That mental effort has been a development over the years.

Next, she tells me about a high-profile engagement as a keynote speaker for Nike. She speaks frankly and honestly as she touches on impostor syndrome. "Who the fuck am I? Here are all these famous players, and I'm supposed to tell them my story?"

But that's exactly what she did. Challenging herself to grow outside her comfort zone is how Nicole honors her commitment to living intensely.

"Risk aversion is really from fear that someone else has experienced. It is passed on to you. Other people's perceptions of classically 'scary' situations develop stereotypes of what 'should' be feared. And how we 'should' react."

Nicole works hard on retraining her brain. She uses meditation, mindfulness, and communication.

"We are our thoughts."

She lives by this.

Ego is a significant contributor to fear.

"It creates fear of shame. Fear of not being good enough."

Nicole still struggles with fear. "We are ultimately wired to feel fear," she says.

She examines this concept with empathy and self-compassion. She meticulously analyzes her visceral responses, remembering to be kind to herself in the process.

"How many times have you been told to focus in class?" she asks. "But has anyone ever told you *how* to focus?"

She is making the point that people are not taught mindfulness, particularly in the US.

"Being able to talk about our aversions, including risk aversions, makes us human. Living in fear manifests that fear."

Despite Nicole's hardships, she found new purpose and meaning by pushing through her comfort zone. Mindfulness and self-compassion allowed her to focus on what can go right, rather than what could go wrong. She shows us that retraining our thinking will enable us to embrace new experiences with courage.

Chapter Ten: The Art of Anticipating Fear - A Skydiver's Guide to Peak Performance

"There's no escaping it," Dan Brodsky-Chenfeld tells me when I ask him to comment on fear.

I was inspired to talk to him after reading his book *Above All Else*. It's a book about fear and overcoming adversity. Dan survived a plane crash, something that gives him a unique vantage point in life.

"The first part of fear is understanding clearly what we are afraid of," he says. "We are scared of things we don't often need to be scared of."

We *react* to fear.

Dan describes his first hot air balloon jump. It took place in the middle of the desert. The balloon was at six thousand. At the time, he'd had about ten thousand skydives under his belt. His logical mind knew there was no reason to be scared, but fear found him.

"I told myself, 'This is not worthy of my fear,' " he recalls.

But what is?

Dan categorizes fear into two distinct entities. In the first, fear has the element of surprise, causing an instinctive response. The second represents fear that can be anticipated.

I dive into both.

He tells me a story about the era of skydiving before audible altimeters were available. "Prior to this, we had instinctive altitude awareness. I could see thirty-five hundred feet as much as I could smell it. I could taste it."

Audible altimeters were already part of the skydiving world when I started jumping. I remember setting mine to forty-five, thirty-five, and twenty-five hundred. Twenty-five hundred feet was my decision altitude. My audible altimeter reminded me that I had to get a parachute above my head.

One day, Dan and his team forgot their audible altimeters. They lost altitude awareness.

"I remember being at fifteen hundred feet, turning around, tracking for half a second, and pulling my parachute."

I get chills down my spine as he unfolds the scenario. I know the dangers of pulling that low: parachute collisions, not having time to deal with a malfunction—a hard landing at best, a fatal landing at worst.

That moment was worthy of Dan's fear. Yet he didn't have time to be scared. He wasn't scared until after he landed. It all happened so fast. He just reacted. Luckily, his training saved his life.

Dan is known as a leading safety expert in the skydiving community.

"I don't take anything for granted. I never become complacent. When I step out of the airplane, I know I will exit safely and get to the ground."

"The power of positive thinking, then?" I ask.

"Not exactly," he explains.

Dan's confidence is in his training. Prior to each jump, he analyzes every possible scenario. He describes visualizing every skydive, acting out the moves, and even picturing the emotions he anticipates will arise.

"Positive thinking is the icing on the cake," he says, "but you have to practice every detail." He sees it in his head, embeds it in his muscle memory. He uses all his senses to recreate the scenario. He intentionally places himself in the midst of fear and visualizes his level of calm under those circumstances.

How does fear manifest in his body?

"Heart racing, palms sweating, feeling sick."

I recognize them all as signs of adrenaline. So does Dan.

After recognizing these physiologic signs, he does not label them as "fear" but instead focuses on their positive effects.

"These are signs of you at your peak performance. You are more alert, quicker. You have the ability to perform better."

He tells me about his team, Arizona Airspeed, and his experience at high-level skydiving competitions.

This is a time when he anticipated fear. "Fear of letting my team down, not performing at my best."

However, he recognized the same physiological responses made his senses sharper. He transcended his fear by reframing his thoughts. He didn't allow fear into this space because it was not worthy of him. Instead, he was able to use the heightened arousal level to his advantage.

Can exposure help?

Dan explains recently coaching an Australian team at a skydiving competition. He told them that anticipating adrenaline-charged physiologic responses as part of the experience is vital. Anticipating these thoughts and reframing them elicits positive feelings.

"It has to be worth overcoming the fear to do what you love so much," he explains. "There's no true fear of failure concerning something you're not passionate about."

The only way to overcome fear is to face it, and immerse yourself in it.

Can these things be taught?

"I absolutely believe that," he tells me.

What is Dan's relationship with fear now?

"I think I have a good system, and it's a work in progress."

They are not mutually exclusive.

Dan's experience as a skydiver and survivor of a plane crash has given him a unique perspective on fear and adversity. He believes that fear can be categorized into two types: fear with an element of surprise, and fear that can be anticipated. He stresses the importance of recognizing the physical responses to fear and reframing them as positive signs of peak performance.

He teaches us that fear is an instinctive response, but we can learn to anticipate it and use it to our advantage. This has led him to become a master skydiver and a leading safety expert in the community.

He shows us that by facing fear head-on and embracing the associated physiological responses, we can turn fear into a powerful tool for personal growth. Exposure and practice are key elements for success.

Chapter Eleven: Controlling Chaos - A Stunt Driver Shares Lessons Learned

Kallie Kerns is a stunt driver. It's in the family. She followed in the footsteps of her dad and her grandpa. But it's not just any ordinary family business. It's a deal with danger, an explosive fusion of exactitude and pandemonium, and one wrong move could mean high-speed disaster. Kallie is a professional stunt driver with a passion for "drifting," an advanced driving technique involving the driver intentionally oversteering, causing the rear wheels to lose traction and slide sideways in the midst of a turn. The driver maintains control of the car during this process, aiming for a smooth and continuous motion, often at high speeds.

This is not news to me. We practically lived at each other's houses growing up. While I was in medical school, she pursued a career in the stunt business.

I ask her to describe "drifting" to me on a fifth-grade level.

"It's controlling a car in an out-of-control state," she explains, citing the *Fast and Furious: Tokyo Drift* movie for context. "It's spinning a rear-wheel drive car or motor vehicle out, then maintaining the spinout and precisely navigating it through a course. Basically, my job is extreme car control."

Precision on the edge of chaos. I'm intrigued. I want to hear about the "oh shit" situations.

"It's a dangerous job," Kallie says, "and people do stupid things."

She describes a scene she witnessed on-set. "The driver lost consciousness from a hard T-bone during a job in downtown LA. The driver's right foot stayed on the throttle and drove toward Video Village. They ended the shot and took the footage while the driver was transported in an ambulance. He and everyone were fine. Thing is, shit happens, and when your job is to crash cars intentionally, sometimes you get a hard lesson in what can go wrong.

"You have to become adept at adapting to the circumstances and making it work. In *Fast 5*, the stunt guy passed out in the vault car because of how hot it was on location, and he was crammed in a motorized sweat box. You have to hone the skill of sorting out all the information you know and relaying only what someone else needs to hear. You have to do it right, and you have to do it right *now*.

"You get better at what could or actually did happen on-set, and there is always a safety meeting for the crew and everyone before the stunts so everyone knows what the protocols are. Because you can't expect things to go right without looking at all the ways they can go wrong, and preparing to adapt to the worst-case scenario.

"We are controlling chaos. And those with experience have seen some shit hit the fan. But guess what? You come back with more knowledge going into the next one with some rock-solid info to add to the equation. Come back smarter and harder."

She recalls some of her own tough decisions.

"Cars can be dangerous pieces of machinery even when operated properly under normal circumstances, let alone when they are operated in an aggressive situation. Because things like speed, timing, surface area, weather, condition of the car, and commitment play a huge part. And since we're often filming on locations like the streets of LA, outside people entering the lockup are a huge hazard when they are not a part of the stunt, nor do they want to be. Bogies. Sometimes you have to sacrifice the car because that's the path of least resistance to avoid potential injuries or the worst-case scenario— somebody losing their life."

The logistics can come down to fractions of a second.

"You realize you have to be your own coordinator," she says, "take charge of your own safety."

Kallie believes there is healthiness in fear.

"If you are completely fearless, you could be the worst fucking safety hazard," she laughs.

Training on a course allows her the luxury to comfortably make mistakes and push her limits.

"Time is money on-set," she explains. "When I'm working, I have to be at my best. I have to adjust to whatever shitty situation I'm given: brakes going out, no power steering to name a few."

She recreates these extreme situations on the training course to challenge the what-if scenario. "When I am on-set, on a job, I do what needs to be done," she says. "At that point, it's not about me, it's about the job."

Teamwork is important to her. She emphasizes that

it's possible to have a great production and great talent, but the job can't get done because of a lack of communication.

"Communication is important. You have to know all the technical details about the car and the course, but you have to communicate succinctly and efficiently. You're thinking of all the math, but you just say, 'Bob, I need to start another five feet back,' because every minute counts."

Kallie concedes that mistakes are required to build experience.

"You can dissect your insufficiencies later. And I always do."

She describes a mental exercise in which she accepts responsibility for anything that goes wrong during a job.

"I just accept, for a moment, everything is my fault. What can I fix? How can I make it better? Rather than shifting blame, I try to see what I can do differently."

This sounds self-critical, but Kallie explains she does it with compassion. Creating a "what-if" worst-case scenario allows her to improve her process.

The entertainment industry, she tells me, is like a war zone at times.

"Life or death can come into play, but more often

than not, it's the fear of the death of your career or self-esteem. Like you're pressured to do something their way, with equipment you're feeling out as you go, with no time to figure it out—people worrying about how much money you cost, constant limitations being added," she says.

"You start to predict how a car is going to react in drifting in order to get a step ahead of it and control it by anticipating what's going to happen. If you are not one step ahead of it, you're usually too late. You have to be humble, willing to learn, and recognize you are always a student. That's how you grow."

I ask Kallie what her take is on the concept of being "fearless."

"It's not about being fearless," she replies, "it's about intentionally exposing yourself to scary situations and practicing being at peace there."

Can anyone do that, or are some people more inclined?

"It's like anything else," she says. "Some people are more inclined, but it's really the individual drive that propels certain people to do it. You have to expose yourself to the adrenaline associated with fear and learn to control yourself under those circumstances. Train to function under those circumstances. But here has to be passion, a greater purpose. That's really key."

Also, you can't become complacent.

"Sometimes, I feel like I'm not cut out for this. And then I remember when I train stunt performers, I walk the walk. I get in the car and I show them it can be done. I show them it's not about just credentials on a piece of paper. It's about making it work."

It comes easier to some, but Kallie believes everyone can be a student. Anyone can change their mindset.

"There are some tough decisions with me and cars," she says. "If you can't work through the fear, it infiltrates safety and work politics. It affects your performance."

She alludes to peak performance under pressure.

"You can sing in the shower all you want, but you may freeze in Carnegie Hall if you've never felt the pressure of everyone watching you and expecting the most out of you. You have to raise the stakes and the adrenaline in practice to really simulate how you perform under pressure.

"So avoid feeling comfortable, otherwise that uncomfortable feeling may come for the first time on-set, and then you realize you'd be a lot more comfortable if you were just willing to fail when it was safe…but on-set, it feels like do or die."

High-pressure situations are a daily occurrence in Kallie's career, and communication and mental preparation are key. Her approach involves accepting responsibility for mistakes, constantly recreating worst-case scenarios in training, and using them as opportunities for growth and improvement. By prioritizing communication with her team, she showcases the skills required to thrive in an industry where every fraction of a second counts.

As she continues to push her limits and refine her skills, Kallie shows us a path to thriving in a field that demands both technical proficiency and mental fortitude.

But she stresses she always goes back to her "why."

"It has to be worth it. Otherwise, there's a soul conflict. There has to be a desire to keep venturing out of your comfort zone."

Chapter Twelve: Decisive Action - The Key to Navigating Emergencies with Confidence

It started as a truly magical morning at Skydive Lodi. The temperature was just right at seventy degrees. Not too hot, not too cold, and the sky was a brilliant shade of blue. A light breeze was blowing through the air, carrying with it the scent of jet fuel and freshly brewed coffee. The perfect combination of thrill and comfort. I was getting ready for a jump with a friend who was coaching me in freefly, a skydiving discipline that involves falling in different orientations as opposed to the traditional belly-to-earth position, such and head down and sit fly. The buzz of excitement was palpable at the drop zone with skydivers preparing for their jumps.

I carefully packed my parachute, taking extra care to "roll the nose," a technique used to soften the parachute opening. Afterwards, I met my friend and we went through our pre-jump routine, discussing the plan and completing our gear check. Everything was in place and ready to go.

We headed out to the runway where the jump plane was waiting for us. We climbed into the plane and took our seats. The plane was packed. The engine roared to life, both familiar and deafening.

As we ascended to 13,000 feet, I felt my nerves beginning to calm. The view from the plane was breathtaking, with the landscape below revealing a vivid patchwork of fields, orchards, and cars on the precariously close freeway. I took a deep breath and focused on my training, letting my mind slip into a state of calm and focus. The plane leveled off and the green light came on, signaling it was time for the exit sequence.

As I stood on the edge of the airplane, I looked down at the vast expanse below. Nothing else mattered except the incredible beauty of the world from an aerial view. The world became still.

We left the airplane at 13,000 thousand feet. We completed the free fall portion, splitting at forty-five hundred feet. After tracking for a thousand feet, I opened at thirty-five hundred.

Immediately, I saw line twists above my head. I attempted to untwist them in the air. I thought I had a good shot. I tried a couple of times but couldn't get the lines straight.

Then my audible altimeter warned me I was at twenty-five hundred feet. I was close to straightening the lines. Should I keep trying to save my main parachute? It would be nice to fly it down so I wouldn't have to hunt for it later.

I was out of time. I chopped it. My right hand ripped off the cutaway handle, and my left hand immediately pulled the reserve handle. My reserve canopy opened above my head.

I did not deviate from my training. I stuck to the hard deck. I have no idea if trying longer to untwist the lines would have saved by main parachute, but I do know that deploying the reserve parachute saved by life.

It was time for analysis back on the ground. If you jump long enough, these things happen. Just like in surgery, complications will inevitably occur. What's important is how you deal with them.

The duration of a skydive is not a time for analysis or self-criticism. It is a time for action. It is certainly not a time for fear.

Fear creates doubt and second-guessing. Fear destroys confidence. Working through these types of situations has fundamentally changed my mindset

I learned to deal with circumstances as they are, focusing on the present and not the past or future. Focusing on process and not emotion.

The inability to face risk creates a prison of inaction. But how can we harness the power of fear and use it to our advantage?

I have asked myself what is on the other side of fear.

I relay to my daughter, Harper, a famous quote: "All ships are safe in harbor, but that's not what ships are built for."

Recently, during a difficult time in her life, one of my colleagues told me, "I've reached my limit on what I will tolerate in this situation."

She was discussing her job. She didn't get the raise that was promised to her the previous year, despite receiving positive feedback from her senior partners, glowing patient reviews, and multiple recognition awards from the hospital.

"What's on the other side of the limit?" I asked her.

Only through transcending our limits do we reach our potential.

Only through transcending our limits do we achieve peace.

I posed a thought exercise. Would she choose this job—these partners, this hospital—if she weren't already there? Or is she hanging onto these things out of fear of loss?

Complacency often masquerades as security. Our intrinsic value is our ability to rebuild. The obstacles in the way, no matter how harsh, can merely be reframed as lessons or opportunities.

Actions are best guided by strength, confidence, and conviction rather than fear and loss.

Every obstacle faced is just another opportunity to grow. Every setback is merely a chance to learn, to improve, and to transcend.

About the Author

Alexandra Kharazi is a cardiothoracic surgeon currently based in Southern California. In addition to her busy practice, she is a mother to the witty and opinionated Harper, who is three going on thirty. Through her work, Alexandra hopes to make a positive impact on others and inspire them to live their best life.

CPSIA information can be obtained
at www.ICGtesting.com
Printed in the USA
BVHW011556200423
662739BV00007B/12